YoungWriters®
— Est. 1991 —

Little Dreamers
Acrostics

Poetic Voices

Edited By Byron Tobolik

First published in Great Britain in 2025 by:

YoungWriters®
Est. 1991

Young Writers
Remus House
Coltsfoot Drive
Peterborough
PE2 9BF
Telephone: 01733 890066
Website: www.youngwriters.co.uk

Foreword

Welcome Reader,

For Young Writers' latest competition Little Dreamers, we asked primary school pupils to write an acrostic poem. They could write about an animal, their favourite person, themselves or something from their imagination – anything at all! The acrostic is a fantastic introduction to poetry writing as it comes with a built-in structure, allowing children to focus on their creativity and vocabulary choice.

We live and breathe creativity here at Young Writers and we want to pass our love of the written word onto the next generation – what better way to do that than to celebrate their writing by publishing it in a book!

Featuring poems on a range of topics, this anthology is brimming with imagination and creativity, showcasing the blossoming writing skills of these young poets. They have brought their ideas to life using the power of words, resulting in some brilliant and fun acrostic poems!

Each awesome poet in this book should be super proud of themselves! We hope you will delight in these poems as much as we have.

Contents

Florence Braunton (6)	62
Lexi Morrow (5)	63
Ezra Atter (6)	64
Ryan Johnson (6)	65
Miller Bexon (6)	66
Jett Baker (6)	67
Luna Cenci (6)	68
Finley Burdett (5)	69
Theodore Carter-Smith (6)	70
Zara Rogers (6)	71
Thomas Czajka (5)	72
Erin Lewis-Norton (6)	73
Edward Oliver (5)	74
Sashvin Sanjeevan (5)	75
Esmae Chappell (5)	76
Scarlett Haddi (5)	77
Ella Green (6)	78
Molly Mills (6)	79
Charlie Luettge (5)	80
Emmett Andrews (5)	81
Harry Bailey (6)	82
Phoebe Dowell (7)	83
Zachary Koltun-Lewis (5)	84
Eva Veasey (6)	85
Alexander Valko (5)	86

Moat Primary School, Lisnaskea

Ollie McCaffrey (7)	87
Aimee Hall (7)	88
Felicity Richmond (6)	89
Alistair Johnston (7)	90
Kaitlyn Johnston (8)	91
Tessa Rutledge (7)	92
George Hall	93
Katie McManus (8)	94
Jenson Higgins (8)	95
Jack Rusk (7)	96
Oscar Farrell (7)	97
Hudson McCauley (7)	98
Grace Kelly (6)	99
Anaya Mehaffy (7)	100
Jacob Henry (6)	101
Glenn Lunny (6)	102

Joel Ebbitt (7)	103
Alex Wilson (7)	104

Seaton Academy, High Seaton

Billy Stoddart (5)	105
Kade Holliday (6)	106
Mason McGovern (6)	107
Ella Nicholson (5)	108
Charlotte Parker (5)	109
Willow Taylor (5)	110
Lydia Tatton (5)	111
Lexie Clark (5)	112
India Sharpe (5)	113
Isla Leggett (5)	114
Seb Courty (5)	115
Evie Lister (5)	116
Noah Stephenson (5), Teddy & Freddy Thomson (5)	117
Ada Ousby (5)	118
Brody Wilson (6)	119
Wrenn Benson (5)	120
Elizabeth Jane Bragg (5)	121
Theo Wilson (6)	122
Noah Rumney (5)	123
Elijah Graham (5) & Reuben	124
Isabelle Taylor (5), Harrison & Reggie Walker (5)	125
Molly Williams (5)	126
Layton McQuire (5)	127

St Francis Catholic Primary School, Shelfield

Olivia Kee (6)	128
Joshua Stanyer (6)	129
James Player (7)	130
Oscar Pusztuk (6)	131
Jack Player (7)	132
Archie Boulton (6)	133
Freddie Williams (6)	134
Evelyn Farnell (7)	135
Martha Holyhead (6)	136
Elsie-Rose Charles (6)	137

The Poems

Zombie Apocalypse

Z ombies bite
O nly chase you
M any little zombies
B ig zombies
I t's scary
E at your brains

A ll little zombies sneak around
P ush down doors
O nly chase you
C reepy
A ll trying to infect
L et's escape
Y uck!
P lease, go away!
S keletons fight with them
E very night.

Mattie Casey (6)
Berkswell C Of E Primary School, Berkswell

Monster Truck

M onster crash
O il leak
N o girls allowed in monster trucks
S uper smash!
T rucks are amazing
E xtreme
R ace!

T raffic
R eally big
U seless wood
C *rash!*
K een engines go.

Blake Chisnall (6)

Berkswell C Of E Primary School, Berkswell

Footballer

F ootball boots

O nside

O ffside

T op of the Premier League

B alls

A mazing goal

L ive football

L ove the players

E pic pace

R eally run at lightning speed.

Theo Nelson (6)

Berkswell C Of E Primary School, Berkswell

Nail Artist

N ice
A mazing
I s kind
L ovely and helpful

A lways amazing
R eally creative
T oday
I s amazing
S pace
T he shiny nails are the best!

Felicity Bird (7)
Berkswell C Of E Primary School, Berkswell

Basketball

B asketball is fun
A mazing
S ee me jump
K eep up with me
E xciting
T ough
B ouncing the ball
A lways fun
L ove basketball
L ooks so good.

Aadam Hussain (6)
Berkswell C Of E Primary School, Berkswell

Footballer

F ootball boots

O ffside

O nside

T -shirts

B oots

A goalpost

L ong shorts

L aps to run

E rupting for a goal

R acing for a shot.

Gregory Matsoukas (7)

Berkswell C Of E Primary School, Berkswell

SpongeBob

S ponge
P lays with you
O ften sad
N eeds water
G oes to the
E pic
B ikini Bottom
O nly if you are good
B ad, he won't play with you.

Morgan Foster (6)
Berkswell C Of E Primary School, Berkswell

Police

P utting robbers in jail

O nly ring if you see a robber

L isten out for robbers

I want to be a policeman

C all the police

E very day, there is a robber outside.

Alexander Cracknell (7)

Berkswell C Of E Primary School, Berkswell

Penalty

P assing is good

E ight goals for me

N ine in the next match

A pass is great

L et us win

T ackle the person

Y ou will never score a penalty.

Freddie Cowling (7)

Berkswell C Of E Primary School, Berkswell

Alligator

A ngry
L onely
L ooks funny
I t is dark green
G rabs people
A cts funny
T reads slowly
O ften mean
R eally squelchy.

Alfie Bent (6)

Berkswell C Of E Primary School, Berkswell

Kittens

K ittens are cute
I love them
T hey are so cute
T hey are so soft
E xcited to get one
N ice, little, soft things
S ofter than a puppy.

Amelie Delaney (6)

Berkswell C Of E Primary School, Berkswell

Teacher

T each children

E ncourage children

A lways kind

C lever

H appy teacher

E xcellent

R un a lot in the corridors.

Martha Conde-Medina (6)

Berkswell C Of E Primary School, Berkswell

Doctor

D eliver babies

O ccupation

C heck-up

T ake care of people

O perations

R eady to make people better.

Autumn Smith (6) & Lucy

Berkswell C Of E Primary School, Berkswell

Bunny

B unnies play
U nique bunnies eat fibre
N ice bunnies jump
N ice bunnies eat broccoli
Y oung bunnies eat grass.

Lilly Gater (6)

Berkswell C Of E Primary School, Berkswell

Kitten

K ind
I love kittens
T hey are cute
T hey are beautiful
E xcited to play
N ew kittens.

Madison Long (6)

Berkswell C Of E Primary School, Berkswell

Space

S un is there
P lanets
A lot of planets
C old and dark in space
E ight planets all around.

Tom Aviss (6)

Berkswell C Of E Primary School, Berkswell

Husky

H uskies run around
U p and down
S pecial kind of dog
K ind
Y ucky pup.

Lottie Prentice (7)

Berkswell C Of E Primary School, Berkswell

Bunny

B ouncy
U ses its snuffly nose
N ice
N eeds food
Y ellow, gold bunny.

Nancy Sherwood (6)

Berkswell C Of E Primary School, Berkswell

Model

M y beautiful me!
O n the stage
D ancing
E pic me
L ook lovely.

Leila Hall (6)

Berkswell C Of E Primary School, Berkswell

Hairstylist

H appily braiding people's hair
A dorable babies coming in
I n a beautiful shop
R especting others
S tyling people that need it
T rying her best to help others
Y awning because she's tired
L isting her jobs
I ncredible skills
S inging beautiful songs
T esting new ideas.

Hajaar Mohamed (7)

Cherry Orchard Primary School, Birmingham

Footballer

F oot kicks the ball

O ut and in the goal

O n the pitch, the player gets it

T eamwork

B all is in the goal

A ll work together, makes the game easy

L ollies for later

L ollies make the players cool down

E nd - one of the players wins a medal

R onaldo!

Dawud Islam (6)

Cherry Orchard Primary School, Birmingham

Firefighter

F ire in a house
I nvestigate
R egularly cook food on their own
E mergency
F ast
I n a fire truck
G ot to go as quickly as they can
H elp cute babies
T hrow water at the house
E ngine
R escue.

Yusuf Ali (6)

Cherry Orchard Primary School, Birmingham

Architect

A mazing job
R edesign what the building needs to have
C areful with what they see
H ouse designs
I mportant ideas
T aking their time
E xplanations
C reation
T aking part in designing.

Nurah Nasir (6)

Cherry Orchard Primary School, Birmingham

Dentist

D irty teeth, so you have to clean them
E quality with other dentists
N eed cleaning at the dentist
T eeth cleaned every day
I clean teeth
S mart teeth cleaning
T eeth are brushed.

Aidan Fazal-Idres (6)

Cherry Orchard Primary School, Birmingham

Builder

B ricks they use to build

U se machines

I nside, fixing people's stuff

L earn how to build and they go home with

D irty clothes

E very day, they use tools and they

R est after.

Younus Hansrod (6)

Cherry Orchard Primary School, Birmingham

Artist

A mazing artwork everywhere
R edo it if mistakes happen
T wenty-three is when I started
I t is my favourite thing
S unsets are the hardest to paint
T alented person, I am.

Ishpreet Dhillon (6)

Cherry Orchard Primary School, Birmingham

Footballer

F ootball skills

O ffside

O nside

T ouches

B icycle kick

A ssist

L isten to the manager

L ikes people

E xcited

R ight foot.

Rajan Badhan (7)

Cherry Orchard Primary School, Birmingham

Firefighter

F ell
I am strong
R un
E verywhere is safe
F ire
I am big
G o into houses
H ot
T ap
E veryone is safe
R ed.

Ayan Osman (6)

Cherry Orchard Primary School, Birmingham

Shopkeeper

S mile

H at

O n the computer

P ay

K ind

E veryone

E very day

P ayment

E quality

R espect.

Aafiya Hussein (6)

Cherry Orchard Primary School, Birmingham

YouTuber

Y ouTubers record videos
O nline videos
U nique
T alk to people
U ltra nice
B eing kind
E xcellent
R ecords.

Karam Sokhi (6)

Cherry Orchard Primary School, Birmingham

Police

P rotect people

O n a mission

L ook at people's cars

I ncredible

C atch criminals

E verybody is cared for.

Dylan Jeed (6)

Cherry Orchard Primary School, Birmingham

Singer

S he sings

I n her high heels

N ice singer

G ives people a lovely performance

E arPods

R eally lovely voice.

Rehn Nahal (7)

Cherry Orchard Primary School, Birmingham

Singer

S mooth voice

I magining her dream

N ice voice

G ood songs

E veryone loves her music

R especting people.

Abigail Murphy (7)

Cherry Orchard Primary School, Birmingham

Builder

B ricks
U sing tools
I n a building
L ight needed
D igging
E xcited
R eady.

Ahmed Ahmed (6)

Cherry Orchard Primary School, Birmingham

Lawyer

L ong journey

A kind person

W e care

Y ou need to be kind

E quality

R espect.

Yusra Hye (6)

Cherry Orchard Primary School, Birmingham

Artist

A mazing at drawing

R elaxing

T alented

I nteresting

S uper calm

T eaches.

Ektha Nahal (7)

Cherry Orchard Primary School, Birmingham

Police

P rison

O bedient

L aw

I nvestigate

C rime

E xcellent.

Amelia Aziz (6)

Cherry Orchard Primary School, Birmingham

Police

P unishment
O peration
L aw
I nside
C rime
E xcellent.

Mikiel Sharif (6)

Cherry Orchard Primary School, Birmingham

Chef

C ooks good food
H ard worker
E ating yummy meals
F antastic chef.

Balraj Ghir (6)

Cherry Orchard Primary School, Birmingham

Bat

B lack bat
A t night, it flaps its wings
T he bat is flying in the dark sky.

Abubakar Umar (6)

Cherry Orchard Primary School, Birmingham

Chef

C ooks food
H ard worker
E xcellent chef
F ries chips.

Nkechi Woodlock (6)

Cherry Orchard Primary School, Birmingham

Vet

V ery careful
E very animal needs love and care
T akes an X-ray.

Taijah Lewis (6)

Cherry Orchard Primary School, Birmingham

Chef

C ooks
H elps
E xcellent food
F eeds customers.

Eva Karra (6)

Cherry Orchard Primary School, Birmingham

Sun

S hiny sun goes
U p in the sky
N ight-time goes bye-bye.

Zaitun Tahiru (6)

Cherry Orchard Primary School, Birmingham

Cat

C hase me
A ll around
T hen hug me.

Esa Muhammad (6)

Cherry Orchard Primary School, Birmingham

Zookeeper

Z ooming cheetahs

O ften eat at the zoo

O ffering food to the animals

K eep releasing animals into the wild

E very day, helping animals

E ating their food

P assionate and kind

E very day, feeding all sorts of animals

R eading books to learn what different animals eat.

Adam Stuteley (7)

Cliffedale Primary School, Grantham

Wonder Girl

W onder Girl
O n Wonder Girl is a blue cape
N aughty villains are stealing toys
D ress is black
E xcited about saving the world
R eally powerful

G oes and helps people
I s going to catch the baddies
R uns so fast
L ooks to help people.

Effie Horner (6)
Cliffedale Primary School, Grantham

Superheroes

S uperhero
U ses a cape to fly
P eople get saved
E pic superhero
R eally good at rescuing
H elping people
E verybody cheers
R eally big green cape
O n his belt is a red stripe
E xciting adventures
S uperhero dives into the water.

Otis Chan (5)
Cliffedale Primary School, Grantham

Zookeeper

Z ookeepers are amazing

O ctopuses are swimming around

O range and black tigers running

K indness all around

E lephants stomping around

E scaping is not allowed

P ut the animals in a cage

E verything we do is to help

R escue the animals.

Olivia Lorne (6)
Cliffedale Primary School, Grantham

Superheroes

S cary and strong
U sing magical powers under the sea
P owerful
E pic fights
R unning
H oping they survive
E pic running animation
R eally fast
O ften fights
E pic salutes
S wimming.

Freddie O'Reilly (6)

Cliffedale Primary School, Grantham

Police

P olice driving through the city to the bank

O fficer Steve is a cop driving to the strong bank

L iving in peace until thieves broke in

I n the bank, it is chaos

C lever cops put the thieves in prison

E nding happily ever after.

Arthur Weavers (6)

Cliffedale Primary School, Grantham

Footballer

F ootball
O n the football pitch
O h, the goalkeeper saved the ball
T eam won the match
B all went into the goal
A team goal
L osing team fell down
L arge block
E yeball
R ed card.

Esa Ilyas (7)
Cliffedale Primary School, Grantham

Bus Driver

B ig red bus
U nique and fun
S eat is nice and comfy

D riving around all day
R eally kind to passengers
I mportant job
V ery friendly
E xcellent
R eally happy being a big bus driver.

Elliott Hart (6)
Cliffedale Primary School, Grantham

Bus Driver

B us driver
U nder the bus is a leaf
S teering wheel

D rives the bus
R oad under the bus
I nside the bus are people
V ery fast bus
E very bus is very shiny
R eally round wheels.

Cooper Brummitt (5)

Cliffedale Primary School, Grantham

Football

F antastic football

O ffside

O nly reds allowed

T eam player

B alls everywhere

A mazing players at Forest

L ook where the person is going with the ball

L ike watching it on TV.

Alex Tupper (5)

Cliffedale Primary School, Grantham

Spiders

S piders are super scary
P lease don't bite me
I t is frightening
D addy spiders have long legs
E xtremely creepy
R eally fun with baby spiders
S cary and poisonous.

Noah Marshall (6)
Cliffedale Primary School, Grantham

Creepy Clowns

C lock
R un
E scape
E at
P otion
Y ucky

C reepy
L ights flickering
O nly me
W eird things
N ight
S ouls.

Alfie Butcher (7)
Cliffedale Primary School, Grantham

Hairdresser

H airbrush

A mazing

I t is fun

R eally short

D ark hair

R eally long

E xcited

S oft

S traight

E veryone

R eally curly.

Maci Dutton (5)

Cliffedale Primary School, Grantham

Rainbows

R ainbows
A lways amazing
I was digging for treasure
N ice people
B ow bear
O ne of my favourite things
W here I have fun
S pecial place.

Spencer Luczak (7)

Cliffedale Primary School, Grantham

Gardeners

G rabs lovely fruit from the

A pple tree

R ainbows

D oes gardening

E very day

N eeds care

E pic flowers

R abbits

S unshine.

Mozan Ismael (6)

Cliffedale Primary School, Grantham

Football

F ootball makes me happy
O wn goals
O ld stadiums
T op of the table
B allboys
A lways running
L ike playing football
L ove the summer.

Freddie Wiseman Chambers (6)
Cliffedale Primary School, Grantham

Mermaid

M agical mermaid
E pic adventures
R ubbish under the sea
M ake sure you pick it up
A mazing swimmers
I t was a success
D ays go past quickly.

Florence Braunton (6)
Cliffedale Primary School, Grantham

Animals

A mazing animals
N eeds help from vets
I love animals
M ake me happy
A lways happy
L ive in habitats
S quirrels are one of my favourites.

Lexi Morrow (5)

Cliffedale Primary School, Grantham

Football

F ootball
O nly play on grass
O ften scoring
T ackles
B attle
A fter scoring, they cheer
L eader
L ooks at the match.

Ezra Atter (6)

Cliffedale Primary School, Grantham

Football

F ootball

O h, awesome football

O h, awesome tackling

T ackling

B ar

A mazing goal

L ord of football

L ove football.

Ryan Johnson (6)
Cliffedale Primary School, Grantham

Football

F ootball
O ver there
O n the pitch
T raining with balls
B ig stadiums
A mazing games
L ove Forest
L ove playing.

Miller Bexon (6)

Cliffedale Primary School, Grantham

Football

F ootball
O wn goals
O ften win
T ough sometimes
B ouncing ball
A ttack
L ove
L ooks easy but it's hard.

Jett Baker (6)
Cliffedale Primary School, Grantham

Animals

A nimals

N ice

I love them

M akes me happy

A nimals are my friends

L ive everywhere

S nakes are my favourite animals.

Luna Cenci (6)

Cliffedale Primary School, Grantham

Football

F ootball
O ver there
O n the pitch
T raining with
B alls
A nd
L ove Forest
L ove playing games.

Finley Burdett (5)
Cliffedale Primary School, Grantham

Doctor

D octors
O perations
C lever doctors
T rying to make people better
O nly sick people go to the doctor
R eally amazing.

Theodore Carter-Smith (6)
Cliffedale Primary School, Grantham

Dancer

D ancing beautifully
A mazing movements
N ice twirls
C areful spins
E xciting performances
R eally good at dancing.

Zara Rogers (6)
Cliffedale Primary School, Grantham

Police

P olice officer
O ften they catch baddies
L ittle police dogs
I n the streets
C ars and vans
E veryone feels safe!

Thomas Czajka (5)

Cliffedale Primary School, Grantham

Unicorn

U nder a rainbow
N ice unicorn
I love it
C orn that pops
O h so lovely
R eally rude
N aughty.

Erin Lewis-Norton (6)
Cliffedale Primary School, Grantham

Vehicle

V ans
E verywhere
H onking their horns
I love them
C an see men
L ooking
E verywhere.

Edward Oliver (5)

Cliffedale Primary School, Grantham

Vehicle

V ans driving

E verywhere

H orns beeping

I like

C ars and

L orries

E verywhere.

Sashvin Sanjeevan (5)

Cliffedale Primary School, Grantham

Dragon

D ragons
R ed wings
A mazing flying skills
G reen spikes
O range horn
N ever fails.

Esmae Chappell (5)

Cliffedale Primary School, Grantham

Dragon

D ragons
R uns quickly
A mazing colours
G reen scales
O range wings
N ice dragon.

Scarlett Haddi (5)

Cliffedale Primary School, Grantham

Spider

S pecial
P ointy legs
I n their web
D ark corner
E nemy
R eally scary.

Ella Green (6)

Cliffedale Primary School, Grantham

Horses

H appy
O ut for a trot
R un fast
S addle
E njoyment
S o much fun.

Molly Mills (6)
Cliffedale Primary School, Grantham

Power

P owerful

O ften strong

W e break through the walls

E pic

R uns really fast.

Charlie Luettge (5)

Cliffedale Primary School, Grantham

Power

P owerful
O ften strong
W e break through walls
E pic
R uns really fast.

Emmett Andrews (5)
Cliffedale Primary School, Grantham

Guitar

G reen
U se a pick
I nstrument
T reat
A wesome
R eally fun.

Harry Bailey (6)

Cliffedale Primary School, Grantham

Vets

V ets helping animals
E very time
T hey are hurt or sick
S o many different ones.

Phoebe Dowell (7)

Cliffedale Primary School, Grantham

Train

T rains
R olling on
A track
I like trains
N ice smoke coming out.

Zachary Koltun-Lewis (5)

Cliffedale Primary School, Grantham

Space

S paceman
P ast the moon
A stronaut
C omet
E arth.

Eva Veasey (6)

Cliffedale Primary School, Grantham

Moon

M idnight
O nly at night
O ften big
N ight-time.

Alexander Valko (5)

Cliffedale Primary School, Grantham

Ollie

O ther people play with me
L earning is cool to do every day
I like numeracy a lot, it's great
V ery good at listening in school
E veryone is kind in my whole family
R eading is good for your brain to learn
new words.

Ollie McCaffrey (7)
Moat Primary School, Lisnaskea

Aimee

A mazing things that I can do
I like kittens, they are my favourite animals
M y birthday is the tenth of April
E mily is my sister's name
E very day when I am tired, I go for a walk.

Aimee Hall (7)

Moat Primary School, Lisnaskea

Felicity

F ull of joy
E yes are brown
L ovely family
I ce cream, I love
C ountryside is my home
I s good at PE
T ake my bunny to my friends
Y ou can be my friend.

Felicity Richmond (6)

Moat Primary School, Lisnaskea

Alistair

A good worker
L iteracy is fun
I like farming
S ports are fun
T ractors are fun
A good farmer
I have never seen an igloo
R eally like cows.

Alistair Johnston (7)

Moat Primary School, Lisnaskea

Kaitlyn

K ind and helpful
A mazing at gymnastics
I like numeracy
T eachers are kind to me
L ovely friend
Y ou are very kind
N ice people do nice things.

Kaitlyn Johnston (8)
Moat Primary School, Lisnaskea

Tessa

T hree sisters to play with
E ating food is good for me
S isters are fun to play with
S inging is fun
A girl who loves to play the piano.

Tessa Rutledge (7)

Moat Primary School, Lisnaskea

George

G ood at playing football
E ating food is good
O ranges are my favourite
R ide on a quad
G o farming with Dad
E yes are blue.

George Hall
Moat Primary School, Lisnaskea

Katie

K ind and helpful
A mazing at singing and dancing
T urtles are my favourite
I am beautiful and cute
E veryone in my family is fun.

Katie McManus (8)

Moat Primary School, Lisnaskea

Jenson

J enson is a good friend
E yes are blue
N ice and funny
S uper good at football
O llie is my friend
N umeracy is fun.

Jenson Higgins (8)
Moat Primary School, Lisnaskea

Jack R

J ack is a very good footballer
A boy with brown hair
C ars are the best
K ind to my friends

R eading is my favourite.

Jack Rusk (7)
Moat Primary School, Lisnaskea

Oscar

O liver is my best friend
S ports are fun
C ars are my favourite toys
A boy with brown hair
R eally good at maths.

Oscar Farrell (7)
Moat Primary School, Lisnaskea

Hudson

H elping is good
U ltra rare Hudson
D ad takes care of me
S uper me
O utside is good
N ot Hudson.

Hudson McCauley (7)

Moat Primary School, Lisnaskea

Grace

G irl with brown hair

R eally good at gymnastics

A brother is nice

C an do a handstand

E yes are blue.

Grace Kelly (6)

Moat Primary School, Lisnaskea

Anaya

A pples are good for you
N ice and kind
A mazing family
Y ou can be my friend
A girl with blue eyes.

Anaya Mehaffy (7)

Moat Primary School, Lisnaskea

Jacob

J okes are funny
A mazing at dodgeball
C ucumber, I love
O ften at Castle Park
B eautiful singer.

Jacob Henry (6)

Moat Primary School, Lisnaskea

Glenn

G ood boy
L ovely family
E ating pizza is good
N umeracy is my favourite subject
N ice boy.

Glenn Lunny (6)
Moat Primary School, Lisnaskea

Joel

J oel is good at literacy
O nly plays football
E yes are blue
L ovely friend.

Joel Ebbitt (7)

Moat Primary School, Lisnaskea

Alex

A lways on the tractor
L ikes eating pizza
E yes are blue
e **X** tra cool.

Alex Wilson (7)

Moat Primary School, Lisnaskea

Space

S pace rocket spins
P lanets spinning, all colourful
A stronauts ride on the rockets
C omets flying past
E arth is in space.

Billy Stoddart (5)

Seaton Academy, High Seaton

Space

S tars are shiny
P lanets are moving
A stronaut is flying in a space rocket
C omets are blue and zooming
E arth is our home.

Kade Holliday (6)
Seaton Academy, High Seaton

Space

S tars are high up
P lanets are really colourful
A stronauts in special helmets
C omets whizz by
E arth is really big.

Mason McGovern (6)

Seaton Academy, High Seaton

Space

S tars shine brightly
P lanets spinning around
A stronauts fly to the moon
C omets shooting down
E verywhere is dark.

Ella Nicholson (5)
Seaton Academy, High Seaton

Space

S tars gleam
P lanet is Earth and we live on it
A stronaut is flying in a rocket
C omets are fast
E arth is our home.

Charlotte Parker (5)
Seaton Academy, High Seaton

Space

S tars are shining
P lanet Earth, we live on it
A stronauts go to the moon
C omets are fast
E arth is our planet.

Willow Taylor (5)

Seaton Academy, High Seaton

Space

S tars are so high up
P lanets are very colourful
A stronauts in special helmets
C omets whizz by
E arth is big.

Lydia Tatton (5)
Seaton Academy, High Seaton

Space

S tars shine bright
P lanets spinning round
A stronauts fly to the moon
C omets whizz by
E verywhere is dark.

Lexie Clark (5)

Seaton Academy, High Seaton

Space

S tars are shining

P lanets are moving

A stronaut is in his space rocket

C omets are fast

E arth is our home.

India Sharpe (5)

Seaton Academy, High Seaton

Space

S hooting stars are zooming
P lanets are spinning
A rocket is flying
C omets are fast
E arth is our planet.

Isla Leggett (5)
Seaton Academy, High Seaton

Space

S tars are so bright
P luto is a dwarf planet
A rocket in space
C omets zoom in the sky
E arth is our home.

Seb Courty (5)

Seaton Academy, High Seaton

Space

S tars are higher up
P lanets are colourful
A stronauts in special helmets
C omets whizz by
E arth is big.

Evie Lister (5)

Seaton Academy, High Seaton

Space

S tars are high up

P lanets are colourful

A stronauts in special helmets

C omets whizz by

E arth is big.

Noah Stephenson (5), Teddy & Freddy Thomson (5)

Seaton Academy, High Seaton

Space

S pace is cool
P lanets are colourful
A stronauts in the stars
C omets flying past
E arth is in space.

Ada Ousby (5)

Seaton Academy, High Seaton

Space

S un is red-hot

P lanets are moving

A re the stars shining?

C an the planets move?

E arth is our home.

Brody Wilson (6)

Seaton Academy, High Seaton

Space

S tars shining
P lanets are moving
A stronauts go to the moon
C omets are fast
E arth is our planet.

Wrenn Benson (5)

Seaton Academy, High Seaton

Space

S tars are in the galaxy
P lanets moving
A liens on planets
C omets are fast
E arth is our planet.

Elizabeth Jane Bragg (5)

Seaton Academy, High Seaton

Space

S tars are shining
P luto has aliens
A rocket is flying
C omets are fast
E arth is our planet.

Theo Wilson (6)

Seaton Academy, High Seaton

Space

S pace rockets

P lanets whizzing

A stronauts go to the moon

C omets buzzing

E arth spinning.

Noah Rumney (5)

Seaton Academy, High Seaton

Space

S pace rockets
P lanets whizzing
A stronauts on the moon
C omets buzzing
E arth spinning.

Elijah Graham (5) & Reuben

Seaton Academy, High Seaton

Space

S pace rockets
P lanets whizzing
A stronauts on the moon
C omets buzzing
E arth spinning.

Isabelle Taylor (5), Harrison & Reggie Walker (5)

Seaton Academy, High Seaton

Space

S un is yellow
P lanets spin
A rocket is flying
C omets are fast
E arth is our planet.

Molly Williams (5)

Seaton Academy, High Seaton

Space

S tars are yellow
P lanets spin
A stronaut
C omets are fast
E arth is our planet.

Layton McQuire (5)

Seaton Academy, High Seaton

Unique

U nderstanding

N eighbourly

I ndependent

Q uick

U pbeat

E njoys playing with my friends.

Olivia Kee (6)

St Francis Catholic Primary School, Shelfield

Unique

U nderstanding people

N eat

I conic

Q uiet

U npredictable

E njoys playing with friends.

Joshua Stanyer (6)
St Francis Catholic Primary School, Shelfield

Unique

U nderstanding

N ice

I ntelligent

Q uiet

U npredictable

E njoys playing.

James Player (7)

St Francis Catholic Primary School, Shelfield

Unique

U nderstanding

N eat

I mproved

Q uick

U npredictable

E njoys scootering.

Oscar Pusztuk (6)

St Francis Catholic Primary School, Shelfield

Unique

U nderstanding
N oble
I conic
Q uick
U pbeat
E njoys going to the park.

Jack Player (7)

St Francis Catholic Primary School, Shelfield

Unique

U npredictable

N ice

I ntelligent

Q uick

U npredictable

E ntertaining.

Archie Boulton (6)

St Francis Catholic Primary School, Shelfield

Unique

U nderstanding

N ice

I mportant

Q uiet

U pbeat

E njoys playing.

Freddie Williams (6)

St Francis Catholic Primary School, Shelfield

Unique

U nforgettable

N ice

I mportant

Q uiet

U pbeat

E njoys drawing.

Evelyn Farnell (7)

St Francis Catholic Primary School, Shelfield

Unique

U nforgettable
N eat
I mportant
Q uiet
U nique
E njoys ballet.

Martha Holyhead (6)

St Francis Catholic Primary School, Shelfield

Unique

U nderstanding

N eat

I mproved

Q uiet

U pbeat

E njoys RSE.

Elsie-Rose Charles (6)

St Francis Catholic Primary School, Shelfield

Unique

U pbeat
N ice
I nviting
Q uick
U nflappable
E xcitable.

Musa Trawally (6)

St Francis Catholic Primary School, Shelfield

Unique

U nderstanding

N ice

I nviting

Q uiet

U pbeat

E xcited.

Frankie Partridge (6)

St Francis Catholic Primary School, Shelfield

Unique

U nique
N eat
I nviting
Q uick
U pbeat
E njoy running.

Mason Hamer (7)

St Francis Catholic Primary School, Shelfield

Unique

U nderstanding

N eat

I conic

Q uiet

U pbeat

E ager.

Karni Trawally (6)

St Francis Catholic Primary School, Shelfield

Unique

U pbeat

N ice

I conic

Q uick

U nforgettable

E ager.

Aleena Frimpong (6)

St Francis Catholic Primary School, Shelfield

Unique

U pbeat

N eat

I ntelligent

Q uiet

U nique

E legant.

Mila Dinham (6)

St Francis Catholic Primary School, Shelfield

Unique

U nflappable

N oble

I conic

Q uick

U pbeat

E ager.

Darcy May Hodson (6)

St Francis Catholic Primary School, Shelfield

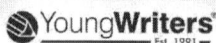

Young Writers
Information

We hope you have enjoyed reading this book – and that you will continue to in the coming years.

If you're the parent or family member of an enthusiastic poet or story writer, do visit our website **www.youngwriters.co.uk/subscribe** and sign up to receive news, competitions, writing challenges and tips, activities and much, much more! There's lots to keep budding writers motivated!

If you would like to order further copies of this book, or any of our other titles, then please give us a call or order via your online account.

Young Writers
Remus House
Coltsfoot Drive
Peterborough
PE2 9BF
(01733) 890066
info@youngwriters.co.uk

**Join in the conversation!
Tips, news, giveaways and much more!**

YoungWritersUK **YoungWritersCW** **youngwriterscw**

youngwriterscw **youngwriterscw-uk**